MARY, TH[E]
CO-RE[...]

by
Michael Haynes

Ad Jesum per Mariam.

NIHIL OBSTAT: Peter Phillips
                 Censor Librorum

IMPRIMATUR: + Mark Davies
                 Bishop of Shrewsbury
                 14th January, 2020

First Edition.
© Michael Haynes, 2019. United Kingdom. All rights reserved.
Cover Photo: Virgin at Prayer by Sassoferrato.
ISBN: 978-0-244-54926-8

RECOMMENDATION

The book "Mary the Motherly Co-Redemptrix", written by Michael Haynes, presents a sound theological reflection on the truth about the unique contribution of the Blessed Virgin Mary to Christ's redeeming work. The book will be a helpful contribution so that the Church and all the faithful may deeper understand this truth, and that there may increase in the spiritual life of the faithful the true devotion to Mary, who is the Mother of God and the Mother of all humankind at the supernatural level.

+ Athanasius Schneider, Auxiliary Bishop of the Archdiocese of Astana.

FOREWARD

This work is the result of prayer and a deep interest in Mary Co-Redemptrix. I decided to study the subject with the aim of writing a little booklet, as I strongly believed, and still do, that a devotion to Mary as Co-Redemptrix should be widely fostered.

Most recently I had the opportunity and grace to pursue this idea and use the topic as my academic thesis at a Catholic university, which would have to be publicly defended. These pages are the result of that painstaking work.

In studying this truth I have discovered a wealth of beautiful truths, but I have also truly learnt just how much I do not know and fallen in love with the Blessed Virgin even more than before. Please God this short and insufficient work will bring others to develop a loving devotion to her, particularly under the title of Co-Redemptrix.

I would like to especially thank my advisor, Fr Crean O.P, for his patient and wonderful advice, as well as my encouraging family for their support and loving help. But most importantly, I must thank Mary, for her guidance throughout this act of devotion to her.

INTRODUCTION

Christ, the Redeemer, is King and Saviour, the crucified God-man who humbled himself on the cross for mankind's redemption. Through His suffering and death on the tree of Golgotha, He opened the gates of Heaven and conquered sin, as foretold in Genesis 3:15. He needed no earthly help, for He is God and thus infinitely powerful. To state otherwise is truly to misunderstand not only God but also His creation. Christ freely offered Himself and became for man "wisdom, and justice, and sanctification, and redemption". (1 Cor 1:30) He chose our Blessed Mother to become the Mother of God, who shared His life with Him through all the jubilations and sorrows. Although a creature of God, Mary was united to Christ's suffering and death in a truly unique and intimate manner. She is honoured with many titles, which furnish her children with aspects of her life on which to dwell and focus, opening up to mankind her union with her Son, in order that man might grow closer to Mary and consequently closer to God. However they are not merely affected titles, for they contain complex truths and wondrous mysteries which carry the utmost import for the Church and the spiritual life of each one of her faithful children. Throughout the centuries, the Fathers and saints have expounded and progressively shed more light upon Marian theology. Holy Mother Church has proclaimed and holds to date, four Marian dogmas: 1) The Divine Motherhood, 2) the perpetual virginity, 3) the Immaculate Conception, 4) The Assumption.[1] The Church also holds other titles of Our Lady in particular regard, each shedding light upon a different aspect of the life of our Blessed Mother and her Divine Son. Amongst the titles of Our Lady which have been consistently taught, lies one of the most beautiful, namely that of Co-Redemptrix. It is this title which further elucidates the union of Mary with her Divine Son, and by implication further unites her children to her and to God. It is more than a mere title, but is indeed a mystery, the content of which is employed by many of the Church Fathers, the great Marian saints, and recently by the Popes - intimated in councils and in individual writings. Holy Mother Church offers Her children the opportunity to approach Mary and venerate Her under the invocation of Co-Re-

---

[1] These were correspondingly defined at the Council of Ephesus in 431, the Lateran Council in 649, by Pius IX in 1854 and by Pius XII in 1950.

demptrix. Coming to Mary means coming unto Christ, and ultimately, by the will of God, to Heaven.

Dr. Miravalle, one of the foremost current defenders of Co-Redemption, explains the term as "the unique and active participation by Mary, the Mother of Jesus, in the work of Redemption as accomplished by Jesus Christ, the divine and human Redeemer".[2] St. Maximilian Kolbe writes about the Annunciation thus: "From that moment God promised a Redeemer and a Co-redemptrix saying: 'I will place enmities between thee and the Woman' ".[3]

To be devoted to Mary under this title and in this way is entirely in concordance with the teaching of the Church, as shall be evidenced by presenting texts from throughout the ages. The collect for the current feast of Our Lady of Sorrows reads, "O God, who willed that, when your Son was lifted high on the Cross, his Mother should stand close by and share his suffering, grant that your Church, participating with the Virgin Mary in the Passion of

---

[2] Dr. Mark Miravalle, *With Jesus - The story of Mary Co-Redemptrix* (Goleta CA, Queenship Publishing, 2003), 10.

[3] St. Maximilian Kolbe, *Scritti*, (Rome, 1997) n.1069 as quoted in Miravalle, *With Jesus*, 217.

Christ, may merit a share in his Resurrection".[4] Hence, starting with the writings of the early theologians and Fathers of the Church, then moving onto the writings from the Middle Ages and the great Marian saints, the work will come to its chronological conclusion with the writings of the recent popes. The teaching and defence of Marian Co-Redemption will thus be tracked from its origins to the full development present in the modern world.

---

[4] *The Roman Missal*, (New Jersey, Catholic Book Publishing Corp, 2011), 807.

REDEMPTION

St. Paul states, "Christ Jesus came into this world to save sinners".[5] He also mentions that, "there is one God, and one mediator of God and men, the man Christ Jesus".[6] Christ is the perfect mediator between God and man since He is both God and man.[7] Consequently, St. Thomas Aquinas notes that the process of redemption "could not be effected either by Adam or by any other purely human being".[8] Objectively, Redemption "is the work of the Redeemer" and is that which effects "the salvation of humanity from the burden of sin".[9] It frees men from the "tyranny of sin", restores the supernatural union between man and God and "was effected by the vicarious atonement and the merits of Christ in His sacrificial death on the Cross".[10] Redemption has a dual aspect of "reparation for the offence caused to God by sin

---

[5] 1 Timothy 1:15, Douay Rheims Version.

[6] 1 Timothy 2:5.

[7] As defined by the Council of Chalcedon, 451.

[8] St. Thomas Aquinas, *Compendium Theologiae*, Chapter 200, (Manchester, New Hampshire, Sophia Press, 2002), 229.

[9] Dr. Ludwig Ott, *Fundamentals of Catholic Dogma*, (Charlotte, North Carolina, TAN Books, 1974),177.

[10] Ott, *Fundamental of Catholic Dogma*, 177.

and the re-establishment of the sinner in the state of child of God".[11] Christ's sacrifice is that of the God-man: "[It is] perfect in itself, from the point of view of the intensity and perfection of love. Its merits are infinite and it does not need to be completed by another holocaust".[12]

As mediator, Christ merits in His own right the graces necessary for the reconciliation of man and bestows them to man.[13] Ott defines merit as "a work completed for the benefit of another on whom it establishes a claim for reward…founded on the work".[14] It can be either *de condigno* or *de congruo* - the former being that which is based upon justice and cannot be merited for another, except by Christ. However, one may merit grace for another in a congruous manner, since, "a man in grace fulfils God's will, and it is congruous and according to the proportion implied by friendship that God should fulfil the man's desire for the salvation of another".[15]

---

[11] Fr. Emil Neubert, *Mary in Doctrine*, (Milkwaukee, Bruce Publishing Company, 1954), 91-2.

[12] Fr. Marie-Dominique Phillippe, *Mystery of Mary - Mary, Model of the growth of Christian Life*, (Houston, Texas, Capital Printing),195.

[13] Neubert, *Mary in Doctrine*, 72-3.

[14] Ott, *Catholic Dogma*, 189.

[15] St. Thomas Aquinas, "Summa Theologiae", 1a 2ae, 114,6. Accessed 13th Feb 2019. https://dhspriory.org/thomas/summa/index.html

Furthermore, "A man's faith avails for another's salvation by congruous and not by condign merit".[16] Christ's redemptive action is simultaneously "satisfactory and meritorious, in as much as, on the one hand, it removes the relationship of guilt between humanity and God, and on the other hand, establishes a claim to recompense on the part of God".[17] The virtuous man can merit *de condigno* for himself and *de congruo* for others.

Condign merit supposes an equality between service and the return and is measured by commutative justice, hence gives a real claim to a reward. In congruous merit there is a lack of proportion between the service and the recompense, and thus claims the reward only on grounds of fairness. By this kind of merit one can merit for others all that one can merit for oneself, such as conversion, the grace of final perseverance and additionally even the first grace for another.

---

[16] Aquinas, "Summa Theologiae", 1a 2ae, 114, 6.
[17] Ott, *Catholic Dogma*, 189.

CO-OPERATION

However, St. Paul also states that "we are God's coadjutors"[18], and that the faithful can "fill up those things that are wanting of the sufferings of Christ".[19] The Apostle does not mean that Christ's sacrifice was lacking, but rather that man must suffer with Christ for the sake of his own salvation and that of others. The concept and language of 'co-operator' in redemption is thus found in Scripture, denoting a subordinate operation with, but under Christ.

Christ's entire life is one of redemption[20] and at Mary's humble *fiat*, "she gave herself entirely to the person and to the work of her Son; she did so in order to serve the mystery of redemption with him and dependent on him, by God's grace".[21] Pope John Paul II teaches that at this moment, Mary gave herself to God with a "full submission of intellect and will".[22] Due to her plenitude of grace and role as the Mother of

---

[18] 1 Corinthians 3:9.

[19] Colossians 1:24.

[20] *Catechism of the Catholic Church - Second Edition*, #517, (Washington D.C, United States Catholic Conference, 2000),130.

[21] *Catechism of the Catholic Church*, #494, 124.

[22] Pope John Paul II, "Redemptoris Mater", #13, in *The Encyclicals of John Paul II*, edited by J. Michael Miller (Indiana, Our Sunday Visitor Publishing Division, 1996).

God, she was "especially predisposed to cooperation with Christ, the one Mediator of human salvation. And such cooperation is precisely this mediation subordinated to the mediation of Christ".[23] Mary's work with Christ is not performed in her own right, but rather "carried out under Christ and in union with Christ from whom it receives all its efficacy".[24] As Neubert explains, Mary's role involved "a certain union of wills, of sufferings, and of self-oblation" in order to do everything.[25] Mary acknowledged her complete dependence upon Christ when her mission was revealed to her at the Annunciation. Miravalle expresses the special union most succinctly, "In a phrase: Mary is 'with Jesus' from the Annunciation to Calvary".[26] This is very true, but even more can be added to that, for Mary is with Christ even after the Crucifixion. She remains by the side of her Son as He is lowered from the cross: she remains on Earth giving her motherly care to the frightened apostles and the early Church.[27] Mary cannot

---

[23] Pope John Paul II, "Redemptoris Mater", #39.

[24] Neubert, *Mary in Doctrine*, 72.

[25] Neubert, *Mary in Doctrine*, 73.

[26] Miravalle, *With Jesus*, 11.

[27] Acts 1:14.

abandon her Son, nor His Church, for she is linked in a bond of deepest love to both. The Church is the mystical body of Christ and Mary as Mother of God and Co-Redemptrix, is forever, 'with Jesus.'

Rev. Scheeben, a prominent nineteenth century theologian, explains that sharing in the merits of Christ "should originally be gained and appropriated for the whole of mankind, by the activity which accompanies the Head's activity in the redemption".[28] This accompanying activity is Mary's, the chief of the members of the Church. Thus "the participation in His merits must necessarily be communicated…by that same member".[29]

The word Co-Redemptrix has its origins in the Latin language and is made up of the two words '*Cum*' and '*Redimere*'. '*Cum*' translates to 'with' in English,[30] denoting one person acting alongside another. Upon consulting any Latin dictionary or other text, one can see that at no

---

[28] Rev. M.J. Scheeben, *Mariology Volume Two*, (St Louis MO, B. Herder Book Co, 1954), 215.

[29] Scheeben, *Mariology Volume Two*, 215.

[30] William Smith & Theophilus Hall, *Smith's English-Latin Dictionary*, (Wauconda, Illinois, Bolchazy-Carducci Publishers Inc, 200) 952. Here *cum* is translated as "together with/in the company of", without any mention of *cum* denoting equality. The same is the case in *Cassel's Latin Dictionary*.

point does the word '*Cum*' ever mean 'equal to' or 'interchangeable', unlike the manner in which a 'co-pilot' refers to one who is interchangeable with the pilot.[31] '*Redimere*' is the verb meaning to 'buy back, set free by payment'.[32] When combined with the female ending of the verb, one can get the meaning "she who buys back with", Co-Redemptrix being a co-operation in Christ's salvific action.

---

[31] It is interesting to note here that some of the entries in Latin Dictionaries have '*cum'* as being used to denote acting under an authority, and taking orders from another.

[32] *Cassell's Latin Dictionary*, rev. by J.R.V. Marchant and Joseph Charles, (New York, Funk & Wagnalls Company, 1956), 473.

MARY IN SCRIPTURE

The appearances of Mary in the Bible, or references to her, are indeed not many, yet a careful examination of these texts will enable one to understand the complex truths contained in them. Certain of these passages will be briefly presented in order to grasp the Scriptural foundations upon which the Fathers built their writings.

The first reference to Mary in Sacred Scripture contains a wealth of Mariological truths, but especially presents Our Lady as Co-Redemptrix. Genesis 3:15 reads, "I will put enmities between thee and the woman, and thy seed and her seed: she shall crush thy head[33], and thou shalt lie in wait for her heel". This passage places Mary in direct opposition to the devil and not merely in a passive manner. It specifically states that she will crush the head of the devil, that she and her seed will be united in their fight against satan. This passage is the basis for all consequent Marian study and presents Mary not

---

[33] Whilst there are various traditions about the translation of this passage as 'she', 'he' or 'it', it is the tradition of the Latin Fathers that the verse be referred to Mary. Pius IX also uses the word thus in *Ineffabilis Deus*. Such teaching is portrayed on the Miraculous Medal also.

only as the Mother of God but also as intimately linked with Him in the process of redemption. Indeed, the Fathers of the Church draw greatly upon this passage in their teaching on Mary as the New Eve. The use of the word 'woman' here is crucial, for it is used to tie together the other appearances of Mary in the New Testament: at the wedding of Cana, at the foot of the Cross and as the woman clothed with the sun in the Apocalypse.

By referring to Mary under the appellation 'woman', Christ does not act in a derogatory manner, but rather is speaking thus "in the exercise of His divine dignity and mission".[34] When Mary is styled as 'woman' it is in the most beautiful and crucial passages relating to salvation, particularly in the protoevangelium[35] and at the foot of the cross. 'Woman' denotes the passages of Marian Co-Redemption in Scripture. This is the case at the wedding feast of Cana, where Mary is responsible for calling to her Son's attention the need for wine at the celebration and Christ addresses her under the title

---

[34] Rev. Scheeben, *Mariology Volume One*, (St Louis MO, B. Herder Book Co, 1954), 11.

[35] The protoevangelium means 'first gospel' and refers to the first mention of the coming of Christ and our Lady as found in Genesis.

"Woman".[36] It is truly fitting that she should be so linked to Him in this very first of His public miracles, for it teaches man about the proper relation which exists between the Mother and her Son. John 2:5 recounts Mary advising the servants that "Whatsoever he shall say to you, do ye". This act is very much part of Mary's Co-Redemptive mission as enacted throughout her life: she sees the problem and then brings those servants to Christ. In like manner she brings her sinful children to Christ, aware that only His death on the cross can save man from sin. But she is always united to Him in this saving act, in a subordinate role.

In the Gospel of St. Luke, one dwells upon the account of the Annunciation. At the very moment of her word of acceptance, '*fiat*', Mary united her will completely to the Divine, consenting and willing "all that her Son's mission will include".[37] Mary studied the scriptures and knew the words of Isaiah, "Behold a virgin shall conceive, and bear a son, and his

---

[36] John 2:4.

[37] Neubert, *Mary in Doctrine*, 74. It is important to realise that had Mary been unaware of the role of the Divine Motherhood then Christ's Redemptive mission would have been undertaken without Mary's informed consent in actions which concerned her.

name shall be called Emmanuel".[38] Mary replied in humble acceptance of the angel's greeting, (Luke 1:38) aware of the true weight of her *fiat*. Indeed, from this moment "that she pronounced her *fiat*, Mary was already in truth the co-operatrix of Christ in the work of our Redemption".[39] This acceptance of the Mother of God is whole and entire, it is necessarily an acceptance of the motherly mission to be Co-Redemptrix. It is a joyful cry of obedient unison to the will of God.

Of course the most poignant appearance of the Blessed Mother in the New Testament is at the foot of the cross. John describes Calvary thus: "There stood by the cross of Jesus, his mother, and his mother's sister, Mary of Cleophas, and Mary Magdalen. When Jesus therefore had seen his mother and the disciple standing whom he loved, he saith to his mother: 'Woman, behold thy son' ".[40] Her position beside the cross is one of suffering and offering. Christ styles her as 'woman', evoking the words of Genesis 3:15; here she is crushing the devil's head and her seed is performing the salvific and

---

[38] Isaiah 7:14.
[39] Neubert, *Mary in Doctrine*, 83.
[40] John 19: 25-26.

redemptive death. This use of 'woman' denotes Our Lady in her role as Co-Redemtrix, fulfilling the words by which she and her Son were promised in Genesis. Marys' position at the foot of the cross is the climax of her Motherly role, for she unites herself so completely to the Divine will that she abnegates her natural desire for Christ's life and wills His salvific death. Thus she has the dual sorrow of witnessing Him in death, whilst lovingly willing Him to die in order that He might conquer sin.

MARY, THE NEW EVE

The early Fathers and theologians of the Church drew their Marian teaching from the words of Sacred Scripture, paying particular attention to Mary as the New Eve. St Paul explains that it is through the New Adam that salvation was wrought for man. (Rom 5:12-21). Just as Adam was accompanied in sin by Eve, so the redeeming Adam must rightly be accompanied by a new Eve. Thus the rich Mariological teaching of 'New Eve' was developed. It is taught by the early Fathers of the Church that "the process of salvation accomplished by Christ, the New Adam, must follow step by step the process of the fall accomplished by Adam, although in an essentially opposite way".[41] As early as the middle of the second century, St Justin the Martyr (†c.165), a great early writer and apologist of the Church, was writing upon the subject of Mariology. Referring to Christ's incarnation, St Justin states that He "became man through the Virgin, that the disobedience caused by the serpent might be destroyed in the same way in

---

[41] Miravalle, *With Jesus*, 65.

which it had originated".[42] Just as sin was caused by a woman, so was sin destroyed by a woman. Following St. Justin and also inspired by St. Polycarp, came St. Irenaeus (†c.202), who is aptly acclaimed as the first true Mariologist. In his work, *Adversus Haereses*, he places Mary and Eve in juxtaposition and contrasts their actions:

> And even as she [Eve] having become disobedient, was made the cause of death, both to herself and to the entire human race; so also did Mary … by yielding obedience, become the cause of salvation, both to herself and the whole human race...thus also it was that the knot of Eve's disobedience was loosed by the obedience of Mary. For what the virgin Eve had bound fast through unbelief, this did the virgin Mary set free through faith.[43]

---

[42] Dr Mark Miravalle, "Mary in the Early Church", Footnote #3. Accessed 5th Feb 2019. http://www.piercedhearts.org/hearts_jesus_mary/heart_mary/mary_early_church_miravalle.htm.

[43] St. Irenaeus, "Adversus Haereses," Volume 3, Chap 22, n4. Accessed on 5th Feb 2019. http://www.newadvent.org/fathers/0103322.htm

With these words, St. Irenaeus presents a clear teaching of Marian Co-Redemption, noting Mary's intrinsic involvement in the process of redemption, but not in any way redeeming under her own power. The important word used is 'obedient', clearly marking Mary as subject to Christ. In *Adversus Haereses*, St. Irenaeus consistently refers to the virginal obedience of Mary as crucial in her role alongside Christ. Having in mind the words of St Paul, "and being consummated, he became to all that obey him, the cause of eternal salvation" (Heb 5:9), Irenaeus uses 'obedience' quite deliberately.[44] Rev. De Margerie observes that for Irenaeus "it signifies that Mary participates in the salvific obedience of Christ on the cross and has participated in it ever since the Annunciation, receiving from her Son the grace of obedience".[45] This presents an important point for this period of history, the linking of the Incarnation with Calvary. The Church teaches that Mary's *fiat* is a complete acceptance "to the entire plan of God" hence

---

[44] Rev. de Margerie states that it is "universally acknowledged" that the saint is referring to Hebrews 5:9.
Dr Mark Miravalle, *Mary - Coredemptrix, Mediatrix, Advocate - Theological Foundations. Vol I.* (Santa Barbara, Queenship Publishing, 1995), 8.

[45] Miravalle, *Mary - Theological Foundations. Vol I*, 8.

she joyfully accepts the sacrifice of Calvary.[46] This humble, obedient and willing co-operation in the Incarnation is exactly how Mary lived her life of co-operative suffering, culminating in her sacrifice at the foot of the cross.

The early Church writer, Tertullian (†c. 250), was keenly aware of how fitting Mary's role is with the plan of redemption: "Into a Virgin was to be introduced the Word of God, the builder-up of life; that by the same sex whence had come our ruin might also be recovered the way to salvation…The fault which the former committed by believing, the latter blotted out by believing".[47] In like manner wrote St. Ephraim (†373), a Doctor of the Church, who contrasts Eve and Our Lady: "Eve wrote a bill of debt and the Virgin paid the debt".[48]

Such teaching is echoed across the Church, with great numbers of the Fathers, Doctors or apologists of the Church turning to Mary as New Eve. For example, St. Gregory of

---

[46] Dr. Mark Miravalle, *Mary, Coredemptrix, Mediatrix, Advocate - Theological Foundations. Vol II*, (Santa Barbara CA, Queenship Publishing Company, 1996), 84. Such teaching can also be found in *Redemptoris Mater*, #13-14.

[47] Tertullian, *De Carne Christi*, ch 17 as quoted in Miravalle, *With Jesus*, 69-70.

[48] St. Ephraem, *On the Institution of the Church*, n11 as quoted in Miravalle, *With Jesus, The Story of Mary Co-Redemptrix*, 70.

Nyssa (†c.395) preached that "Eve brought in sin by means of a tree; Mary, on the contrary, brought in Good by means of the tree of the Cross".[49] This once again presents the theme of Mary accepting all at the Incarnation and consequently at the cross.

So also said St. Jerome (†c.420), who wrote how "death came through Eve, but life has come through Mary".[50] He also refers to the bond of unitive suffering between Christ and His mother, "Every torture inflicted on the body of Jesus was a wound in the heart of the Mother".[51]

The great bishop of Hippo and Doctor of the Church, St. Augustine (†430), continued the work of the Patristic period in furthering the understanding of Marian theology. He taught that Mary brought the salvific life which Eve had done away with through her sin. Since by a woman death came, so by a woman came life:

---

[49] St. Gregory of Nyssa, *Sermon for the Nativity of Christ*, as quoted in Miravalle, *Mary - Theological Foundations Vol I*, 18.

[50] St Jerome, "Letter 22 To Eustochium," Paragraph 21. Accessed 5th Feb 19. http://www.newadvent.org/fathers/3001022.htm

[51] St. Alphonsus de Liguori, *The Glories of Mary*, (London, Burns, Oates & Washbourne Ltd, 1868), 445. No further precise reference is given except the original latin verse.

It is a great sacrament that, as death came to us by a woman, life was born to us by a woman; so that in both sexes, feminine and masculine, the devil, being conquered, might be tormented, as he had glorified in the downfall of both. He would not have been adequately punished had both sexes been freed, but we had not been freed by both.[52]

St. Augustine declared that, "The cross and nails of the Son were also those of His Mother; with Christ crucified the Mother was also crucified".[53]

It is the common belief and teaching of the Patristic age, that Mary was involved in a unique and privileged manner in the redemption. By contrasting her to Eve, they argue for the fittingness of Mary as being the New Eve who accompanies the New Adam in His salvific action. Mary's humility and obedience are central themes in the exposition of her as the New Eve. Thus occurs the re-ordering of the world, with Mary becoming the new and spotless Eve to

---

[52] St. Augustine, *De Agone Christiano*, ch 22, as quoted in Miravalle, *With Jesus*, 71.
[53] Liguori, *The Glories of Mary*, 445. No further precise reference is given except the original latin verse.

usher in salvation. Just as Eve had been the pinnacle of the creation of the world, so also is Mary the highest creature of God. Whilst Eve opened her heart to sin through listening to the deceitful words of the devil, Mary accepted the fullness of God's will for her and by doing so brought redemption instead of corruption. The openness of her pure and humble heart to the will of God, contrasts directly to the proud and corrupted heart of Eve who hearkened only to the tempter.

The Fathers do not use the term 'Co-redemptrix' explicitly, but rather teach the underlying truths of the term and acclaim Mary as New Eve. They outline how Mary is constantly with and co-operating with Jesus throughout His life from the Incarnation to Calvary, but particularly at the cross, which is the essence of Marian Co-Redemption.

THE FLOURISHING OF MARIAN THEOLOGY: MARY AS CO-REDEMPTRIX

The famous saints and scholars who emerged during the medieval period unpacked the truths contained in the Fathers' writings and greatly developed the understanding of Our Lady and specifically her role in the redemption. Indeed, so great is the number of saints and mystics who wrote about Co-Redemption, that the attention here will be given to but a few.

The first recorded use of the title, 'Redemptrix', is found in a French psalter which originates from the tenth century, and reads "Holy Redemptrix of the world, pray for us".[54] This litany uses the feminine form of 'Redeemer', but without any attempt to equate Mary with Christ.

Styled as the *Doctor Mellifluus,* St. Bernard's (†1153) great devotion to Mary, especially as Co-Redemptrix, is quite evident from his vast collection of Marian works. In his second sermon on the *Missus Est*, St. Bernard draws so heavily from the Fathers that one would imagine

---

[54] Miravalle, *With Jesus*, 82. Referring to *Litanies des saintes*, now housed in the chapter library in Salisbury Cathedral.

himself to be reading them: "God gave a woman in exchange for a woman…one who instead of the fruit of death, shall give you [humanity] to eat of the tree of life, and who, in place of the poisoned food of bitterness, will bring forth the fruit of everlasting sweetness".[55] In these words he continues in the vein of the Fathers, yet in his next lines he begins to elaborate their deeper meaning: "O woman singularly venerable! admirable among all women! thou who hast satisfied for thy parents, and restored life to their posterity".[56] Here, the key words, 'satisfied' and 'restored' are employed, denoting that Mary is critically involved in the salvific action. The saint is preaching that Mary, by her involvement with Christ at Calvary, has thus satisfied for sin. He refers back to the prophecy in Genesis by stating that it is fitting that "the enemy who had been victorious over the human race by means of a woman should by another woman himself be overcome".[57] Clearly, Mary is being described as being active in the redemption, satisfying for sin and overcoming the devil. All this is written

---

[55] *Sermons of St. Bernard on Advent and Christmas*, (London, R & T Washbourne, Ltd, 1909), 35-6.

[56] *Sermons of St. Bernard on Advent and Christmas*, 36.

[57] *Sermons of St. Bernard on Advent and Christmas*, 37.

however, in full knowledge of her complete dependence upon God. Later in the homily, St. Bernard states that "the power of Christ broke the strength of the Evil One, and the might and wisdom of God confounded the devil's malice and craft".[58] He is not attempting to proclaim Mary as any sort of equal to God, or even able to redeem man by her power, but is observing her role, with and under Christ, in redemption.

St. Bernard gave great weight to the teaching of Mary as Co-Redemptrix by explicitly using the term of co-suffering, or compassion. In his sermon for the Sunday during the octave of the Assumption, St. Bernard states:

> One can well say, indeed, that a sword pierced your heart, o blessed Mother, for it was only through your heart that it could penetrate the flesh of your Son…His pain, like a violent sword, has thus passed through your heart, and we can call you, with reason, more than a martyr, since in you the sense of compassion has prevailed

---

[58] *Sermons of St. Bernard on Advent and Christmas*, 43.

so strongly over that passion endured by the body.[59]

Holy Mother Church expresses its agreement with the text by using this section in the Office of Readings for the feast of Our Lady of Sorrows!

A friend of St. Bernard, Arnold of Chartres, composed a line in which he described the scene on Calvary in the most beautiful language: "Whoever then was present on the Mount of Calvary might see two altars, on which two great sacrifices were consummated; the one in the body of Jesus, the other in the heart of Mary".[60] His words served to inspire and were used by both St. Alphonsus and Pope St. John Paul II.

Moving from the *Doctor Melifluus* to the seraphic doctor, the same teaching regarding Mary is intensified and the language made consistently more clear and precise. St. Bonaventure

---

[59] St. Bernard, "Sermon pour le dimanche dans l'octave de l'Assomption de Marie," paragraph 14. Accessed on 9th Feb 2019. http://www.abbaye-saint-benoit.ch/saints/bernard/tome03/homsaints/saints021.htm

[60] Arnold of Chartres, as sourced in St. Alphonsus Liguori, *The Glories of Mary*, 445. St. Alphonsus mis-attributes the quotation to St. John Chrysostom.

(†1274), hailed as the greatest Franciscan theologian, wrote prolifically in both philosophy and theology. He furthers the teaching of St. Bernard, concerning Mary as the New Eve and her role alongside Christ in the Redemption: "That woman [Eve], drove us out of Paradise and sold us; but this one [Mary] brought us back again and bought us".[61] Not only is the language of New Eve present here, but also the explanation of her action, the buying back again. St. Bonaventure is demonstrating that Mary is directly in opposition to Eve's sin, drawing out the truths contained in the writings of earlier centuries. In his seven conferences on the gifts of the Holy Spirit, which have been used as a handbook on theology of grace for the Franciscan Order ever since, the saint speaks of her as offering satisfaction for the sins of man.

St. Bonaventure's words not only amply demonstrate his own ardent love for the Mother of God, but also the great depth of the understanding of Marian Co-Redemption at that time. His words run in a similiar vein to Arnold of Chartres, except that Bonaventure depicts only one altar: "there was but one altar - that of

---

[61] St. Bonaventure, *De donis Spiritus Sancti*, collatio 6; 14. as quoted in Miravalle, *With Jesus*, 94.

the cross of the Son, on which, together with this Divine Lamb, the victim, the Mother was also sacrificed; …O Lady, where are thou? near the cross? Nay, rather, thou art on the cross, crucified, sacrificing thyself with thy Son".[62]

These few lines are awash with the truth of Marian Co-Redemption. In unpacking the text, one can see that St. Bonaventure refers to only one altar, that of Christ, thus denoting that it is only through and in His power that redemption occurs. But one can also see that in the union of suffering, the Mother was also freely offered upon the altar of the cross, consequently being inseparably involved in the redemption.

St. Bonaventure provides further evidence of such teaching in his *Little Psalter of Our Lady*, a series of psalms and canticles addressed to the Mother of God. In psalm thirty-one of this collection, he states, "Blest are they whose hearts love thee, O Virgin Mary, their sins will be mercifully washed away by thee".[63] In psalm forty-six, "For she is the gate of life, the door of

---

[62] St. Bonaventure, *De Stim. Div Am p. i. c. 2.* as quoted in Ligouri, *The Glories of Mary*, 445.

[63] St. Bonaventure, "The Psalter of the Blessed Virgin Mary," Psalm 31. Accessed on 11th Feb 2019. https://www.ewtn.com/library/SOURCES/PSALTER.TXT

salvation, and the way of our reconciliation".[64] Both of these lines demonstrate the gravity of the role which Mary had, for St. Bonaventure is attributing to her the washing away of sins and proclaiming that she is the way of man's salvation. Most important though, is a line found in his fifty-first psalm, which reads: "Why dost thou glory in malice: O malignant serpent and infernal dragon? Submit thy head to the Woman: by whose power thou art plunged into hell".[65]

St. Bonaventure additionally composed canticles to Our Lady in the manner of those found in the Bible and in these also, one can find passages acclaiming Mary's role in salvation: "Behold, Lady, thou art my saviour… Exalt her and praise her, all the human race: because the Lord my God has given to thee such a mediatrix".[66]

These are but a few selections of St. Bonaventure's great treasury of writings devoted to Our Lady. In both these saints' works one can especially see the link to the patristic era, with

---

[64] St. Bonaventure, "The Psalter of the Blessed Virgin Mary," Psalm 46.

[65] St. Bonaventure, "The Psalter of the Blessed Virgin Mary," Psalm 51.

[66] St. Bonaventure, "The Psalter of the Blessed Virgin Mary," Canticle on model of Isaiah.

regards to the language they employ about Mary. St. Bernard expresses the teaching of Co-Redemption quite clearly and St. Bonaventure builds upon this clarity in his teaching, sometimes not as succinctly as his predecessor, but with an evident acceptance and understanding of the doctrine.

The great theologian and doctor of the Church, St. Thomas Aquinas (†1274), cherished a devotion to the Blessed Mother and thus amongst his writings can be found further evidence of the continued development of the understanding of Marian Co-Redemption. To begin with, it is necessary to turn to the pages of the *Summa Theologiae* where St. Thomas discusses the matter of the mediator between God and man. He restates the words of the Bible and the belief of all mentioned above, namely, that "Christ alone is the perfect mediator of God and men, inasmuch as, by His death, He reconciled the human race to God".[67] With this truth affirmed, the angelic doctor next states that "nothing hinders certain others from being called mediators, in some respect",[68] thus opening up his

---

[67] Aquinas, "Summa Theologiae", 3a. 26, 1.
[68] Aquinas, "Summa Theologiae", 3a. 26, 1.

later discussion of a Christo-centric Marian redemption: Christ has redeemed man, not Mary, yet she is united to Him in His work. He notes the intimate union between Christ and His Mother, such that just as Christ was possessed of the plenitude of grace, so also "the Blessed Virgin Mary received such a fulness of grace that she was nearest of all to the Author of grace; so that she received within her Him Who is full of all grace; and by bringing Him forth, she, in a manner, dispensed grace to all".[69] This passage clearly presents Mary as being the vessel through which grace is given to the world. By her *fiat* at the Annunciation, Mary gave "to God the free gift of her obedience", thus enabling all to enter into the covenantal relationship with God.[70]

However, it is in his commentary on the Angelic Salutation that the Marian teaching of Aquinas begins to come to the fore, as he elucidates the lines of the first half of the Hail Mary. In similar phrasing to that seen in the *Summa*, Aquinas utters a powerful line regarding her fullness of grace and work in salvation:

---

[69] Aquinas, "Summa Theologiae", 3a. 27, 5 ad1.
[70] Aquinas, "Summa Theologiae", 3a. 30, 1.

The plenitude of grace in Mary was such that its effects overflow upon all men. It is a great thing in a Saint when he has grace to bring about the salvation of many, but it is exceedingly wonderful when grace is of such abundance as to be sufficient for the salvation of all men in the world, and this is true of Christ and of the Blessed Virgin.[71]

Here St. Thomas is linking Christ with Mary in salvation by declaring that their grace was sufficient to save mankind from the punishment due to its sin.

Yet again, the saint unites Mary with her Divine Son, in the work of bestowing grace and redeeming sinful man. In turning to Scripture Aquinas states that it is:

Through her {Mary} we conquer the devil. '*He went down to him with a rod, and forced the spear out of the hand of the Egyptian*' (2 King 23:21)…that is out of the hand of the devil…Mary is our beloved Queen, for through her power we are set free from

---

[71] St. Thomas Aquinas, *The Angelic Salutation*, translated by Joseph Collins. Accessed on 13th Feb 2019. https://dhspriory.org/thomas/english/AveMaria.htm

the hands of all our enemies. '*The Lord will send forth the sceptre of thy power. Rule thou in the midst of thy enemies.*' (Ps109:2).[72]

Aquinas' distinction between *de condigno* and *de congruo* merit, and the explanation of one person meriting for another, are key for Pope Pius X, as referenced later. In distinguishing between these two kinds of merit, Aquinas explains the theological intricacies regarding that which Mary can merit. *De congruo* is the kind of meritorious action which Mary performs, "based on the appropriateness of recompense for her joint suffering with Jesus".[73] She unites her will to Christ, making a full offering to God - Aquinas states that "it is congruous that when a man makes good use of his power God should by His super-excellent power work still higher things".[74]

St. Thomas does not present the reader with such a wealth or clarity of texts as some other saints, but what he does demonstrate is the understanding of the time - that Mary is the means of grace being bestowed upon the world.

---

[72] Rev. Mezard, *St. Thomas Aquinas Meditations*, (Columbus Ohio, 1940), 103. No further precise reference is given.

[73] Miravalle, *With Jesus*, 155.

[74] Aquinas, "Summa Theologiae", 1a 2ae, 114, 6.

Through his characteristic, exact language, the Angelic Doctor teaches the unity of Mary and Christ in the salvific bestowal of grace upon man and the plenitude of grace which Mary has.

St. Alphonsus de Ligouri (†1787) combines the works of almost all the Marian writings which had been written before him, for in his *Glories of Mary*, he fills the pages with quotation after quotation from the early Fathers up to the most recent saints. Written during the time when the Jansenists were plaguing the Church and ridiculing Marian devotion, it is heralded as one of the greatest works of devotion to Our Lady, perhaps surpassed only by St. Louis de Montfort's writings. Amongst the many beautiful passages, St. Alphonsus' teaching on Co-Redemption is found most clearly in his reflections upon Mary's dolours. He first states how Mary endured the most grievous martyrdom, in union with her Son: "So also did Mary, in all things like unto her Son, endure her martyrdom throughout her life".[75] After quoting many clear statements regarding the co-suffering of Our Lady, St. Alphonsus declares, "Thus was our Blessed Lady, through the compassion of her loving

---
[75] Ligouri, *The Glories of Mary*, 405.

heart for her Son, scourged, crowned with thorns, insulted, and nailed to the cross".[76] The saint fills his pages with lines of pious and deeply moving insights into the life of Mary, and the word 'compassion', or others describing her joint suffering and martyrdom, are abundantly found in the text.[77] He demonstrates how her offering with her Son won for man salvation: "She incessantly offered the life of her Son to the Divine Justice for our salvation. Therefore we know that by the merits of her dolours she coöperated in our birth to the life of grace; and hence we are the children of her sorrows".[78] At the end of his reflection on the death of Jesus, the saint closes with a prayer, in which he utters the line, "Mother of Mercy, I hope, first, through the death of my Redeemer, and then through thy sorrow, to obtain pardon and eternal salvation".[79] St. Alphonsus leaves no doubt in the reader's mind as to the teaching regarding Our Lady - she is quite clearly held to be the one who cooperated with Christ in the suffering and

---

[76] Ligouri, *The Glories of Mary*, 410.

[77] In the section on her fifth dolour, only seven pages long, St. Alphonsus mentions Mary's compassion or co-suffering at least seven times.

[78] Ligouri, *The Glories of Mary*, 448.

[79] Ligouri, *The Glories of Mary*, 450.

death on the cross. He also presents the very beautiful image of Mary with the symbol of her martyrdom:

> To show the sufferings endured by other martyrs, they are represented with the instruments of their torture…Mary is represented with her dead Son in her arms; for He alone was the instrument of her martyrdom, and compassion for Him made her the Queen of martyrs.[80]

This simple reflection is firstly a sign of the depth of understanding the saint has regarding Mary, but also presents the unmistakable truth, namely that Mary's sacrifice is of herself and her Son. It also demonstrates that although Alphonsus' Marian devotion is extremely great, he always views her as a creature subject to God. He composes a prayer dwelling upon the sorrowful mother at the cross, in which he appeals to Mary thusly, "I beseech thee, by the agony which thou, my most loving Mother, didst endure together with thy dying Son".[81]

---

[80] Ligouri, *The Glories of Mary*, 598.
[81] Ligouri, *The Glories of Mary*, 657.

In writing upon the purification of Our Lady, St. Alphonsus states that:

> Mary, then, having by the merit of her sorrows, and by sacrificing her Son, become the Mother of all the redeemed, it is right to believe that through her hands Divine graces, and the means to obtain eternal life, which are the fruits of the merits of Jesus Christ, are given to men.[82]

Hence in Alphonsus' lines, the golden age of Mary recognised as the Co-Redemptrix has definitively arrived.

The greatest Marian saint of all, St. Louis de Montfort (†1716), presents his Mariology principally in his treatise, *True Devotion to Mary*, in which he taught the necessity of approaching Mary since she is so intimately united with God. His theology can be summarised in the phrase, *Ad Jesum per Mariam*. One cannot begin to truly understand Montfort's Mariology without working from a prior acceptance and understanding of Co-Redemption, since his *True Devotion* is written based upon this teaching. This

---

[82] Ligouri, *The Glories of Mary*, 366.

much is evident from the opening pages where the saint describes the union between Christ and Mary:

> He has glorified His Independence and His Majesty, in depending on that sweet Virgin, in His Conception, in His Birth, in His presentation in the Temple, in His Hidden Life of thirty years, and even in His death, where she was to be present, in order that He might make with her but one same sacrifice, and be immolated to the Eternal Father by her consent.[83]

The lives of Mary and her Son are linked and so they remain in the great sacrifice, both joined in one oblation to the Father. St. Louis-Marie here teaches that Mary's entire life was one of sacrifice, culminating at Calvary. Further on he writes that "it is by Mary that the salvation of the world has begun, and it is by Mary that it must be consummated".[84] Montfort's thought is rooted in Mary's *fiat*, so that her work in the Incarnation is completed by her work at

---

[83] St. Louis-Marie de Montfort, *True Devotion to the Blessed Virgin*, (London, Burns, Oates & Washbourne, 1904), 9.

[84] de Montfort, *True Devotion to the Blessed Virgin*, 28

Calvary, for just as she was essential for the Incarnation, so was she for the Crucifixion. This is visible in his continuation of the thought of the Church Fathers, as he describes Mary saving by her humble obedience: "What Eve has damned and lost by disobedience, Mary has saved by obedience…Mary, being perfectly faithful to God, has saved all her children and servants together with herself, and has consecrated them to His Majesty".[85] Indeed, the saint's famous method of consecration to Jesus through Mary is established upon Mary being thus united with Christ in Redemption: he writes that in turning to Mary one ultimately turns to Christ, for just as she was the means by which He came to man, she is the "means which we must make use of to go to Him".[86] Mary is this vessel of mediation due to her Co-Redemptive role on Calvary. This beautiful Marian spirituality is that which influenced later Popes, who shall be discussed below.

    Whilst the focus of these pages has been given to the most prominent Co-Redemptrix theologians, there are many other saints and mystics whom it would be foolish to overlook. Amongst these are the revelations to St. Bridget

---

[85] de Montfort, *True Devotion to the Blessed Virgin*, 33.
[86] de Montfort, *True Devotion to the Blessed Virgin*, 51.

of Sweden from Jesus and Mary, as well as the writings of Peré Salmeron along with Sts. Catherine of Siena and Robert Bellarmine.

The development made in the understanding and promotion of Marian Co-Redemption during this period is very great. The statements made during the Patristic era, particularly regarding Mary as the New Eve, are extrapolated and expanded, with the theological explanations of Co-Redemption becoming ever more precise. Eventually, Sts. Alphonsus and Louis-Marie develop their entire Mariological thought with Co-Redemption as their central theme.

PAPAL TEACHINGS

With such an overwhelming weight of teaching present in the Church, it was only a matter of time before the Popes became involved in the matter of Marian Co-Redemption. The number of statements is quite remarkable and thus only those most weighty will be examined here.

In defining the dogma of the Immaculate Conception, Pius IX issued the Apostolic Constitution *Ineffabilis Deus* (1854), containing a synthesis of Marian teaching regarding the Mother of God, of which some naturally pertained to her as Co-Redemptrix. He refers back to the Fathers and their exegesis of Genesis 3:15, stating that: "They also declared that the most glorious Virgin was Reparatrix of the first parents, the giver of life to posterity".[87] Here the Pope uses the word which was employed by many medievals and equated with Co-Redemptrix. His teaching was furthered by his great successor, Pope Leo XIII, renowned for his multitudinous encyclicals and also styled as the 'Rosary Pope'. In *Jucunda Semper* (1894), the Pope

---
[87] Pope Pius IX, "Ineffabilis Deus", 1854. Accessed on 25th Feb 2019. http://www.papalencyclicals.net/pius09/p9ineff.htm

refers to the rosary as being a thorough meditation upon Mary as the Co-Redemptrix throughout her life: "In it [the rosary], all the part which the Virgin played in acquiring the salvation of men returns, as set forth and as having its effect now".[88] In his brief meditation upon the Crucifixion, Leo XIII notes the proximity of Mary to the Cross and the meaning of such nearness: "there stood by the Cross of Jesus His Mother, who, in a miracle of charity, so that she might receive us as her sons, offered generously to Divine Justice her own Son, and died in her heart with Him, stabbed with the sword of sorrow".[89] Further he continues, in remarking how she is the mediator of man's salvation: "To thee we lift our prayers, for thou art the Mediatrix, powerful at once and pitiful, of our salvation".[90] In 1901, the Pope taught that, "Every time we, with the angel, greet Mary as full of grace…we remember all the most singular merits by which She has

---

[88] Pope Leo XIII, "Jucunda Semper", 1894, Accessed 9th April 2019. http://w2.vatican.va/content/leo-xiii/la/encyclicals/documents/hf_l-xiii_enc_08091894_jucunda-semper-expectatione.html It is worth noting that the official English translation uses the word 'co-Redemptress'.

[89] Pope Leo XIII, "Jucunda Semper" #3.

[90] Pope Leo XIII, "Jucunda Semper" #8.

become a partaker with her Son Jesus in the Redemption of humanity".[91]

Pope St. Pius X continued the use of such language in his encyclical, *Ad Diem Illum* (1904), which was released to mark the fiftieth anniversary of *Ineffabilis Deus*. The pontiff mentions that she has the office of, "presenting [Christ] for the sacrifice" and that "from this community of will and suffering between Christ and Mary she merited to become most worthily the Reparatrix of the lost world".[92] By drawing from St. Bernard and the spirituality of St. Louis de Montfort, he describes Christ as the source but Mary as the channel, who "merits for us *de congruo*, as they say, what Jesus Christ merits for us *de condigno*, and she is the supreme Minister of the distribution of graces".[93] This technical language is also that of St. Thomas as outlined earlier and hence the Pope is denoting that "Mary merits for humanity in the order of 'fittingness' or congruous merit, that which Jesus

---

[91] Apostolic Letter *Parta humano generi*, "Acta Sanctae Sedis", 34 (1901) 194. Accessed 25th Feb 2019. http://www.vatican.va/archive/ass/index_en.htm

[92] Pope St. Pius X, "Ad Diem Illum", 1904, section 12, in *The Papal Encyclicals 1903-1939* (United States of America, The Pierian Press, 1990), 13-14.

[93] Pope St. Pius X, "Ad Diem Illum", section 14, 14.

merits for us in the order of 'justice' or strict condign merit".[94]

On another occasion, in response to a *dubium* regarding the weight of the feast of the Seven Sorrows of Mary, the Congregation of Rites declared the wish that, "the devotion of the Sorrowful Mother may increase and the piety of the faithful and their gratitude toward the merciful Co-Redemptrix of the human race may intensify".[95] Such usage of the title is a great development in the promulgation of the doctrine of Co-Redemption. Since the reply was issued from the Congregation and recorded in their official acts, it lends the title yet further weight. Indeed, in 1913 the Holy Office granted a partial indulgence to a prayer of reparation to Our Lady, which ended with the words, "I bless thy holy Name, I praise thine exalted privilege of being truly Mother of God, ever Virgin, conceived without stain of sin, Co-Redemptrix of the human race".[96] Here the Holy Office quite liberally uses the term in an indulgenced prayer,

---

[94] Miravalle, *With Jesus*, 155.

[95] "Acta Sanctae Sedis", 41 (1908), 409.

[96] "Acta Apostolicae Sedis", 6 (1914), 108. Accessed 25th Feb 2019. http://www.vatican.va/archive/aas/index_en.htm

very positively expressing the implicit approval of the devotion and the title.

Pope Benedict XV greatly promoted the devotion to Our Lady under this title, by clearly explaining her role in the redemption. In his letter, *Inter Sodalicia* (1918), he wrote on the unity of sacrifice of Mother and Son:

> With her suffering and dying Son, Mary suffered almost to the point of death; she renounced her maternal rights over Him and, for the purpose of appeasing the Divine Justice inasmuch as it was dependent upon her, she offered up her Son so that it can truly be said of her that with her Son she ransomed mankind.[97]

However, it fell to Pius XI to first use the title Co-Redemptrix in a papal address. In speaking to a group of pilgrims from Vicenza in 1933, he uttered these words:

> By necessity, the Redeemer could not but associate his Mother in his work. For this reason we invoke her under the title of

---

[97] Benedict XV, *Inter Sodalicia*; "Acta Apostolicae Sedis", 10 (1918), 182.

Coredemptrix. She gave us the Savior, she accompanied him in the work of Redemption as far as the Cross itself, sharing with Him the sorrows of the agony and of the death in which Jesus consummated the Redemption of mankind.[98]

In 1934 and 1935 he repeated the explicit use of the term twice, clearly demonstrating his ardent belief in Mary's role.[99]

Whilst not a primarily Marian document, *Lumen Gentium* (1964) contains a great deal of teaching regarding Mary. Before the Second Vatican Council, a multitude of requests were made by bishops regarding Mary's mediation, with fifty bishops specifically requesting a definition of Mary as Co-Redemptrix.[100] A note sent in response to this petition stated that any such definition would not occur, due solely to ecumenical reasons, not any theological problems. The note reads:

---

[98] Pius XI, "Allocution to Pilgrims from Vicenza, Italy." November 30, 1933, *L'Osservatore Romano*, Dec. 1, 1933, 1, as quoted in Miravalle, *With Jesus*, 158.

[99] As recorded in Miravalle, *With Jesus*, 158-59 and Miravalle, *Mary - Theological Foundations Vol I*, 227.

[100] Miravalle, *With Jesus*, 167.

"Certain expressions and words used by supreme Pontiffs have been omitted, which, in themselves are absolutely true, but which may be understood with difficulty by separated brethren. Among such words may be numbered the following: 'Co-redemptrix of the human race' ".[101]

Hence whilst a definition did not occur, a condensed presentation of Mariology is nevertheless contained in the final chapter of *Lumen Gentium*. Chapter eight details a brief history pertaining to Co-Redemption theology, starting with the Scriptures and then moving onto the Fathers and their teaching on Mary as New Eve. The Council Fathers write that:

Embracing God's salvific will with a full heart and impeded by no sin, she devoted herself totally as a handmaid of the Lord to the person and work of her Son, under Him and with Him, by the grace of almighty God, serving the mystery of redemption. Rightly therefore the holy Fathers see her as used by God not merely in a passive way, but as freely cooperating

---

[101] Miravalle, *With Jesus*, 171.

in the work of human salvation through faith and obedience.[102]

The document also refers to Mary as the "cause of salvation" and employs the words of St. Irenaeus regarding Mary being the New Eve as found in the *Adversus Haereses*.[103] Only a few lines later, the document continues in the best lines of Co-Redemptive thought:

> After this manner the Blessed Virgin advanced in her pilgrimage of faith, and faithfully persevered in her union with her Son unto the cross, where she stood, in keeping with the divine plan, grieving exceedingly with her only-begotten Son, uniting herself with a maternal heart with His sacrifice, and lovingly consenting to the immolation of this Victim which she herself had brought forth. Finally, she was given by the same Christ Jesus dying on

---

[102] Second Vatican Council, "Dogmatic Constitution on the Church - Lumen Gentium", Section 56. Accessed 28th Feb 2019. http://www.vatican.va/archive/hist_councils/ii_vatican_council/documents/vat-ii_const_19641121_lumen-gentium_en.html

[103] "Lumen Gentium", 56.

the cross as a mother to His disciple with these words: 'Woman, behold thy son'.[104]

Lumen Gentium describes Mary's role in light of the concept of *de congruo* merit, when it discusses her mediation being not only pleasing to God, but also aiding to "foster the immediate union of the faithful with Christ".[105] So also does the text state that Mary was united with Christ throughout His life, but pivotally on Calvary:

> She conceived, brought forth and nourished Christ. She presented Him to the Father in the temple, and was united with Him by compassion as He died on the Cross. In this singular way she cooperated by her obedience, faith, hope and burning charity in the work of the Saviour in giving back supernatural life to souls. Wherefore she is our mother in the order of grace.[106]

---

[104] "Lumen Gentium", 58.
[105] "Lumen Gentium", 60.
[106] "Lumen Gentium", 61.

The entirety of the chapter is awash with Co-Redemptive language. The Council Fathers teach that her maternity began with her *Fiat* and lasts until the end of time. They also refers to Mary as having a "salvific duty" and bringing to man the gifts of salvation.[107] Through the heavy use of the language of co-operation, *Lumen Gentium* thus implicitly teaches the doctrine without using the actual term, yet quoting terms from previous Papal Co-Redemptrix teaching: "Advocate, Auxiliatrix, Adjutrix, and Mediatrix".[108]

Whilst the Council avoided using the term, Pope John Paul II used the title prolifically in his writings and addresses. Greatly inspired by the Marian spirituality of St. Louis-Marie, the Pope penned the encyclical *Redemptoris Mater* (1987), in which he states: "Mary is perfectly united with Christ in his self-emptying… Through faith the Mother shares in the death of her Son, in his redeeming death".[109] He frequently uses words referring to her sharing in the life and death of Christ and teaches that "inter-

---

[107] "Lumen Gentium", 62

[108] "Lumen Gentium", 62. The original footnote in the document quotes Leo XIII's *Adjutricem*, Pius X's *Ad Diem illum*, as well as Pius XI and XII.

[109] John Paul II, "Redemptoris Mater", 18, 371.

ceding for all her children, the Mother cooperates in the saving work of her Son, the Redeemer of the world".[110] The Pope released this Marian encyclical nine years into his papacy, but in the years prior to this he had already referred to Mary under the title of Co-Redemptrix many times. Most notable among those is his homily in Guayaquil, Ecuador in 1985, in which he discourses on Mary "having suffered for the Church"[111]:

> The silent journey that begins with her Immaculate Conception and passes through the 'yes' of Nazareth, which makes her the Mother of God, finds on Calvary a particularly important moment. There also, accepting and assisting in the sacrifice of her son, Mary is the dawn of Redemption…Crucified spiritually with her crucified son, she contemplated with heroic love the death of her God… In fact, at Calvary she united herself with the sacrifice of her Son that led to the foundation of the Church…Nevertheless, as she was in a special way close to the Cross of

---

[110] John Paul II, "Redemptoris Mater", 40, 396.
[111] Miravalle, *Mary - Theological Foundations. Vol II*, 123.

her Son, she also had to have a privileged experience of his Resurrection. In fact, Mary's role as Coredemptrix did not cease with the glorification of her Son.[112]

In reading the text of this homily, one becomes very clearly acquainted with a theological explanation of Scripture and the words of *Lumen Gentium*. But a few months later, the pope gave a homily on Palm Sunday, in which he commended devotion to Mary: "May Mary our Protectress, the Co-Redemptrix, to whom we offer our prayer with great outpouring, make our desire generously correspond to the desire of the Redeemer".[113] In a general audience given on October 25, 1995, the pontiff gave a brief history of the development of Co-Redemptive teaching in the Church where he traced its origins from the Fathers through to the time of St. Bernard. In another audience given in 1996, he noted the woman of the Apocalypse as Mary at the Cross, and also repeated Mary's role as the New Eve: "This [Rev 12:2] refers to the mother of Jesus at

---

[112] John Paul II, "Homily at Sanctuary of Our Lady of Guayaquil", Jan 31 1985, *L'Osservatore Romano*, English edition, March 11, 1985, 7 as quoted in Miravalle, *Mary - Theological Foundations Vol II*, 123.

[113] John Paul II, *L'Osservatore Romano*, English edition, April 9 1985, 12, as quoted in Miravalle, *Mary - Theological Foundations Vol II*, 124.

the Cross, where she shares in anguish for the delivery of the community of disciples with a soul pierced by the sword…It was fitting that like Christ, the new Adam, Mary too, the new Eve, did not know sin and was thus capable of co-operating in the Redemption".[114]

John Paul II delivered a series of seventy catechetical teachings on Our Lady between 1995 and 1997, of which a key part was the General Audience of April 2 1997 where he gave a very insightful meditation on Mary's compassion:

> With our gaze illumined by the radiance of the resurrection, we pause to reflect on the Mother's involvement in her Son's redeeming passion, which was completed by her sharing in his suffering. Let us return again, but now in the perspective of the Resurrection, to the foot of the Cross where the Mother endured 'with her only-begotten son the intensity of his suffering, associated herself with his sacrifice in her mother's heart, and lovingly consented to the immolation of this victim which was

---

[114] John Paul II, *L'Osservatore Romano*, English edition, June 5 1996, 11, as quoted in Miravalle, *With Jesus*, 203.

born of her.' ... In her heart reverberates all that Jesus suffers in body and soul, emphasising her willingness to share in her Son's redeeming sacrifice and to join her own maternal suffering to his priestly offering.[115]

Pope John Paul II not only uses the title Co-Redemptrix with great frequency, but he also writes and preaches explaining Co-Redemptive theology. Influenced by St. Louis, he is devoted to Mary as being intimately united with Christ in the redemptive act and thus recognises that closeness to Mary is closeness to God.

The Catechism of the Catholic Church, as compiled during the pontificate of Pope John Paul II, also contains the teaching of Marian Co-Redemption. In passage 411, the text presents the teaching of the Church Fathers regarding Mary as being the New Eve who accompanies the New Adam. This is continued as the Catechism draws from St. Irenaeus and teaches that Mary united herself completely to the Divine Will "in order to serve the mystery of redemption with him and dependent on him, by

---

[115] John Paul II, *L'Osservatore Romano*, English edition, April 9 1997, 7 as quoted in Miravalle, *With Jesus*, 204. Internal quotation from *Lumen Gentium* #58.

God's grace".[116] The text refers to *Lumen Gentium* #56 as well as St. Thomas Aquinas, and quotes that Mary "co-operated through free faith and obedience in human salvation".[117] Mary is the vessel through which the Holy Spirit brings man to a knowledge of God and "into communion with Christ".[118] Thus interwoven into the text of the Catechism, lie the Co-Redemptive teachings of the Fathers of the Church, alongside the Marian passages of *Lumen Gentium*.

Clearly, the writings and teachings, both of the Popes and other organs of the magisterium, not only add substantial weight to the doctrine of Co-Redemption, but also considerable clarification and meaning. By addressing Our Lady under the title and writing so beautifully, the Popes not only inspire further devotion to Mary thus, but also present deep, theological conclusions about the doctrine. Some Popes use the title very deliberately, whilst others use it with a certain reverent ease; both manners serve to build upon the teachings which they refer to and to promote the doctrine of Marian Co-Redemption in contemporary society. As Père Neubert

---

[116] *Catechism of the Catholic Church*, #494.
[117] *Catechism of the Catholic Church*, #511.
[118] *Catechism of the Catholic Church*, #726.

wrote in 1954, the Popes clearly credit Mary with "ransoming us in union with her Son, although by a title inferior to His; and of distributing to men all the graces of the Redemption - a consequence of her participation in the Redemption".[119] If these lines were true under the reign of Pius XII, they are surely much more credible in light of later teachings.

---

[119] Neubert, *Mary in Doctrine*, 80.

OBJECTIONS TO CO-REDEMPTION

Despite the teaching of the popes and saints already presented, some questions might still be raised. Many of these have already been addressed in the course of the text, but one question which should be noted is as follows: The cause of merit cannot be the recipient of merit; however, Mary was redeemed by Christ and so how could she co-operate in the Redemption since she was redeemed by that self-same Redemption?

In response to this, one must first state that Mary had no part in that aspect of Redemption which pertained to her. Her redemption is due solely "to the merits of salvation through the Redeemer".[120] Mary does not co-operate in her redemption for she cannot redeem herself: "no one can merit for himself the first grace".[121] Consequently, "Christ first ransomed his own mother" before mankind, so that, "Mary already benefitted, in advance, from the fruits of the sacrifice and acted in the capacity of

---

[120] Scheeben, *Mariology Volume Two*, 43.
[121] Aquinas, "Summa Theologiae", 1a 2ae, 114, 5.

a ransomed creature".[122] But that act of redemption which is directed to others, she freely co-operates and shares in. The single redemptive act of Christ thus has two applications and intentions: "The first application effecting the Immaculate Conception of Mary so as to form and prepare the "New Eve"; the second application effecting the Redemption of the human family in which Mary can participate meritoriously and fruitfully".[123]

Neubert refers to the fact that Mary "had been predestined with Christ before the rest of men by a priority of importance".[124] This is also found in a verse used in the divine office for the feasts of the Annunciation and Our Lady of Good Counsel - "He elected her and pre-elected her".[125] In *Ineffabilis Deus*, Pius IX declared that Mary had been preserved from all stain of sin from the moment of her conception, due to a special grace of God and "in view of the merits of Jesus Christ".[126] Explaining the

---

[122] Rev. Jean Galot S.J, "Mary Co-redemptrix: Controversies and Doctrinal questions", Accessed on 14th March 2019. http://www.christendom-awake.org/pages/marian/5thdogma/galot.htm

[123] Miravalle, *Mary - Theological Foundations Vol II*, 30.

[124] Neubert, *Mary in Doctrine*, 86.

[125] Neubert, *Mary in Doctrine*, 86. "*Elegit eam et praeelegit eam*". *Diurnale Romanum*, 1961.

[126] Pius IX, "Ineffabilis Deus".

words of *Ineffabilis Deus*, Scheeben writes that Mary was from the moment of her conception liberated and redeemed by Christ.[127] Fr. Most explains that Mary received preventative redemption: "the grace she received at her conception was given in anticipation (Latin *praevenire*) of Christ's merits, which earned that grace".[128] Mary "was redeemed 'by the grace of Christ' ", both before all and more perfectly than all.[129] This anticipated redemption thus explains her ability to act as Co-Redemptrix on Calvary: "being pre-elected she was by that very fact pre-redeemed in His intention, so that she with Christ might redeem the rest of mankind".[130]

Since Mary was by this grace fitted to bear God in her womb she was also fitted to "add her action to His at that moment when He actually redeemed us".[131] Miravalle and O'Carroll also observe that redemption, as pertaining to Mary, is different to that of the rest of humanity, since she was without sin due to Christ's

---

[127] cf Scheeben, *Mariology Volume Two*, 43.

[128] Fr. William Most, "Mary's Immaculate Conception", Accessed 13th March 2019. https://www.ewtn.com/faith/teachings/mary-a2.htm

[129] Ott, *Catholic Dogma*, 199.

[130] Neubert, *Mary in Doctrine*, 86.

[131] Neubert, *Mary in Doctrine*, 86.

merits and thus did not need His satisfaction for any sin of hers.[132] *Lumen Gentium* teaches that Mary was "predestined from eternity by that decree of divine providence which determined the incarnation of the Word to be the Mother of God" and thus "cooperated by her obedience, faith, hope and burning charity in the work of the Saviour in giving back supernatural life to souls".[133] Having received the merits of Redemption from the moment of conception she was uniquely able to participate in some way in Christ's action. By distinguishing between a priority in nature and time, one can thus explain Mary's ability to co-operate with Christ, whilst still depending upon His saving merits. For despite the simultaneous sacrifice of Mary and Christ, His "was intrinsically superior in nature and could by the Father be made a principle of merit for her independently of the time factor".[134] She is the redeemed Co-Redemptrix, having, "already benefited, in advance, from the fruits of the sacrifice" and thus able to ransom

---

[132] Miravalle, *Mary - Theological Foundations Vol II*, 29. Rev. Michael O'Carroll, *Mediatress of all Graces*, (Maryland, Newman Press, 1958), 190.

[133] *Lumen Gentium*, #61.

[134] O'Carroll, *Mediatress of all Graces*, 190.

mankind with her Son.[135] Thus Galot states that Co-Redemption means the "foreseen redemption of Mary, but not the foreseen fulfillment of the redemption of mankind… the unique situation of the mother who, while having received a singular grace from her own Son, cooperates with him in the attainment of salvation for all".[136]

    Another objection raised is that the term Co-Redemptrix seems to place Mary upon equal terms with God, or at the very least lead to confusion. This can best be answered by offering an explanation of the term as has been done here, including the exact definition of the term. In light of such an explanation, it is evidently false to teach that Co-Redemption has ever meant anything other than Mary's subordinate cooperation in the plan of God. Rather, the word is based upon the Pauline exposition of how the faithful can co-operate with Christ, as has been mentioned above when referring to 1 Cor 3:9. One must turn also to the words of St. Louis de Montfort, who reminds the reader at the start of *True Devotion* that Mary is as nothing compared to God, and owes her very existence to Him. St.

---

[135] Galot, "Mary Co-redemptrix".
[136] Galot, "Mary Co-redemptrix".

Alphonsus's book *The Glories of Mary* is very evidently written in full knowledge that she is only a creature of God; He alone can redeem. When one has offered a true explanation of the term, alongside such an exposition of the Church's constant teaching, any confusion regarding Co-Redemption should be removed.

However, one should not shy away from teaching Mary as the Co-Redemptrix. If one avoids this title and the accompanying truths, sadly one can never come to know and love the Mother of God properly. Co-Redemption is the crucial aspect of Mary's life, intrinsically linked in her role as the Mother of God and the Church. To ignore Mary as Co-Redemptrix leads to rejecting her as the Mediatrix of graces and can lead to a weakening in a proper understanding of her Divine Motherhood. Pope Pius XII teaches in his encyclical, *Ad Coeli Reginam*, that just as Christ is King because He is our God and Redeemer, so also "the Most Blessed Virgin is queen not only because she is Mother of God, but also because, as the new Eve, she was associated with the new Adam".[137] Mary's Divine

---

[137] Pope Pius XII, *Ad Coeli Reginam*, #38. Accessed on 13th June 2019. http://w2.vatican.va/content/pius-xii/en/encyclicals/documents/hf_p-xii_enc_11101954_ad-caeli-reginam.html

Motherhood and Queenship is crucially linked to her role as Co-Redemptrix.

Others take 1 Timothy 2:5-6[138] and argue against Co-Redemption thusly. This argument is indeed based upon Scripture, but is a one-sided understanding of Scripture. John Paul II observes how just prior to these lines, St. Paul calls for prayers and intercessions to be made for men, but as prayers are a form of mediation, he is clearly teaching of human action under Christ's. The pontiff answers the objection in a Papal address:

> "We recall that Mary's mediation is essentially defined by her divine motherhood. Recognition of her role as mediatrix is moreover implicit in the expression "our Mother," which presents the doctrine of Marian mediation by putting the accent on her motherhood.... In proclaiming Christ the one mediator (cf. 1 Tim. 2:5-6), the text of St. Paul's Letter to Timothy excludes any other parallel mediation, but not subordinate mediation. In fact, before emphasizing the one exclusive mediation

---

[138] "For there is one God, and one mediator of God and men, the man Christ Jesus: Who gave himself a redemption for all".

of Christ, the author urges 'that supplications, prayers, intercessions and thanksgivings be made for all men' (2:1). Are not prayers a form of mediation? Indeed, according to St. Paul, the unique mediation of Christ is meant to encourage other dependent, ministerial forms of mediation.... In truth, what is Mary's maternal mediation if not the Father's gift to humanity?".[139]

Scripture presents instances of the faithful being obliged to participate in something that is also 'one', exclusive and dependent entirely upon Christ. For example, Christ is the only Son of God and there is also only one priesthood of Christ. Yet the faithful are adopted sons of God, a priestly people, and so the Church calls men to share in that which is one and unique in Christ. It is in light of such teaching that man has the sharing in the one mediation of Christ but completely dependent upon Him.

---

[139] John Paul II, Papal Address, Rome, October 1, 1997, *L'Osservatore Romano*,
1997, 41. As quoted in http://www.christendom-awake.org/pages/marian/5thdogma/co-redemptrix1.htm Accessed on 16th April 2019.

Following such an explanation, some try to state that Mary's co-operation with God is no different to that of any other man. However, her co-operation is truly unique for only she participated in the objective, historical and universal Redemption as enacted on the cross. Indeed only she was able to do so, since having received prevenient redemption, only she was without stain of sin and hence in any way able to offer her action alongside Christ. John Paul teaches in *Redemptoris Mater*, that Mary's mediation is due to her Divine Motherhood, hence her mediation is completely unique.[140]

Many objections to Mary as Co-Redemptrix stem from a poor understanding of the concept and a reluctance to teach it. With careful explanation and teaching, such problems can be avoided, enabling the faithful to be given the opportunity to draw closer to Mary in a more intimate union.

---

[140] Redemptoris Mater #39.

CONCLUSION

Through her suffering and union with Christ, Mary merited *de congruo* that which Christ merited *de condigno*. In light of these terms, the title of Co-Redemptrix can be explained thus:

> In the power of the grace of Redemption merited by Christ, Mary, by her spiritual entering into the sacrifice of her Divine Son for men, made atonement for the sins of men, and (de congruo) merited the application of the redemptive grace of Christ. In this manner she co-operates in the subjective redemption of mankind.[141]

In light of this, one can say that Marian Co-Redemption means that "we can say we have been saved first and principally by Christ and secondarily by the action of Mary in subordination to the action of Christ".[142] Mary's unique action is due to her Divine Motherhood, on which her participation in the Redemption is founded. St. John Damascene applies Psalm 44:13 to her and teaches that all her action is due to her Mother-

---

[141] Ott, *Catholic Dogma*, 213.

[142] Neubert, *Mary in Doctrine*, 73.

hood; "the glory of the Theotokos is from within, the fruit of her womb."[143]

Whilst she is the Immaculate Conception, the purest of all creation, she remains still a creature of God made by Him to return to him. St. Louis Grignion de Montfort writes these words on the Blessed Virgin:

> I avow with all the Church, that Mary, being but a mere creature that has come from the hands of the Most High, is in comparison with His Infinite Majesty less than an atom; …[God] never had, and has not now, any absolute need of the Holy Virgin for the accomplishment of His will and for the manifestation of His glory. He has but to will in order to do everything.[144]

At no stage in the development of the devotion and subsequent dogmas about Mary is there any evidence of a deviation of worship to her which is due to God alone. Fr Neubert states that, "Christ's action is independent, not requiring

---

[143] St. John Damascene, "Homily on Nativity of the Holy Theotokos", Para 9. Accessed Nov 2018 https://www.johnsanidopoulos.com/2016/09/oration-on-nativity-of-holy-theotokos.html

[144] de Montfort, *True Devotion to the Blessed Virgin*, 7.

another for its completion; it is totally sufficient in itself. On the other hand, Mary's action is dependent, having efficacy only through its union with Christ's."[145] Co-Redemption has no meaning without Redemption; those who in their zeal might attribute to Mary any greater role in the redemptive sacrifice contrary to that taught above are in fact not adding glory to her name, but doing quite the opposite. It is clear therefore that Mary is not in any way equal to God, completely subject and dependent upon Him, yet intimately united with Him in a bond of suffering love.

The doctrine of Marian Co-Redemption can thus be traced from its origins in Sacred Scripture, through the exposé of the Fathers regarding the New Eve, thence to the glory of the Marian flourishing in the Middle Ages, culminating with the magisterial teaching of the Popes. With the immense growth in understanding of the title, one can say that the "co-effecting of our salvation by Mary's cooperation in Christ's sacrifice must be regarded as theologically certain, and not simply as a pious opinion".[146] By her co-suffering and union with Christ the Redeemer,

---

[145] Neubert, *Mary in Doctrine*, 86.
[146] Scheeben, *Mariology Volume Two*, 237.

Mary, "gave satisfaction to God for sin, merited grace, and thus redeemed the world, because of the fact that she shared in giving and providing the ransom".[147] This is a fact which Holy Mother Church has even recognised in her liturgy, for in 1482 the feast of the 'Compassion of Our Lady' was added to the Roman Missal and later moved to the Friday preceding Palm Sunday by Benedict XIII.[148] Her most intimate union with her Divine Son necessitates that she partake in the Redemption alongside Him, since, united as they are, how could she do otherwise? The sword prophesied by Simeon is foretelling her Co-Redemptive act: "Mary's fate is intimately linked to that of her Son. That is why her soul must be pierced by a sword. Mary's soul must be tortured".[149] By uniquely partaking in Christ's Redemption as His Mother, Mary can fulfil her *fiat*, humbly responding to God's call to be the Co-Redemptrix.

---

[147] Scheeben, *Mariology Volume Two*, 225.

[148] Fr. William Saunders, "The Feast of Our Lady of Sorrows" Accessed 14th March 2019 https://www.catholiceducation.org/en/culture/catholic-contributions/the-feast-of-our-lady-of-sorrows.html

[149] Phillippe, *Mystery of Mary*, 130.

In 2017, the International Marian Association[150] issued this statement as part of a longer appeal to the Pope:

> Not only is the Co-redemptrix term theologically acceptable in articulating the intimacy and complementarity between the divine Redeemer and his immaculate human mother, but the title is actually necessary to properly denote and signify in a single term the providentially designed unity between Jesus and Mary, God-man and human woman, New Adam and New Eve, Redeemer and Co-redemptrix, in the historic work of Redemption.[151]

Indeed, the Church has consistently taught that Mary is the Co-Redemptrix through Her Fathers, saintly theologians and pontiffs. Through the cult of devotion to the Co-Redemptrix, as briefly evidenced above, one can

---

[150] 'The **International Marian Association** (IMA) comprises theologians, bishops, clergy, religious, and lay leaders who seek to promote full Marian truth and devotion throughout the world'. internationalmarian.com

[151] Theological Commission of the International Marian Association, "The Role of Mary in Redemption", section 10. Accessed 15th March. https://internationalmarian.com/sites/marian/files/uploads/documents/the_role_of_mary_in_redemption_1.pdf

observe that Co-Redemption is a doctrine evidently contained in the faith of the Church. Mgr. Calkins states appropriately that: "it does not seem to me that at this point a Catholic is free to deny that Mary has collaborated intimately in the work of the Redemption wrought by her Son or that she has made an altogether unique contribution to that work".[152] Mary cannot be properly understood if one does not seek to understand her role as Co-Redemptrix of humanity, always united with Christ, subordinated to Him in a union of love and sacrifice.

---

[152] Miravalle, *Mary - Theological Foundations II*, 145.

Bibliography:

"Acta Apostolicae Sedis". Accessed 25th Feb 2019. http://www.vatican.va/archive/aas/index_en.htm

"Acta Sanctae Sedis". Accessed 25th Feb 2019. http://www.vatican.va/archive/ass/index_en.htm

Aquinas, St. Thomas. *Compendium Theologiae*. Manchester, New Hampshire, Sophia Press, 2002.

Aquinas, St. Thomas. "Summa Theologiae". Accessed 13th Feb 2019. https://dhspriory.org/thomas/summa/

Aquinas, St. Thomas. "The Angelic Salutation," translated by Joseph Collins. Accessed on 13th Feb 2019. https://dhspriory.org/thomas/english/AveMaria.htm

Augustine, St. *De Agone Christiano*, as sourced in Miravalle, Dr. Mark. *With Jesus - The story of Mary Co-Redemptrix*. Goleta CA, Queenship Publishing, 2003.

Bernard, St. "Sermon pour le dimanche dans l'octave de l'Assomption de Marie". Accessed on 9th Feb 2019. http://www.abbaye-saint-benoit.ch/saints/bernard/tome03/homsaints/saints021.htm

Bonaventure, St. *De donis Spiritus Sancti*, collatio 6; 14. as sourced in Miravalle, Dr. Mark. *With Jesus - The story of Mary Co-Redemptrix*. Goleta CA, Queenship Publishing, 2003.

Bonaventure, St. *De Stim. Div Am p. i. c. 2.* as quoted in Ligouri, St Alphonsus. *The Glories of Mary*, London, Burns, Oates & Washbourne Ltd, 1868.

Bonaventure, St. "The Psalter of the Blessed Virgin Mary" Accessed on 11th Feb 2019. https://www.ewtn.com/library/SOURCES/PSALTER.TXT

Cassell's Latin Dictionary, revised by J.R.V. Marchant and Joseph Charles. New York, Funk & Wagnalls Company, 1956.

Catechism of the Catholic Church - Second Edition. Washington D.C, United States Catholic Conference, 2000.

Damascene, St. John. "Homily on Nativity of the Holy Theotokos". Accessed Nov 2018 https://www.johnsanidopoulos.com/2016/09/oration-on-nativity-of-holy-theotokos.html

de Montfort, St. Louis-Marie. *True Devotion to the Blessed Virgin*. London, Burns, Oates & Washbourne, 1904.

Ephraem, St. *On the Institution of the Church*, as sourced in Miravalle, Dr. Mark. *With Jesus - The story of Mary Co-Redemptrix*. Goleta CA, Queenship Publishing, 2003.

Galot S.J, Rev. Jean. "Mary Co-redemptrix: Controversies and Doctrinal questions". Accessed on 14th March 2019. http://www.christendom-awake.org/pages/marian/5th-dogma/galot.htm

International Marian Association, Theological Commission of the. "The Role of Mary in Redemption". Accessed 15th March. https://internationalmarian.com/sites/marian/files/uploads/documents/the_role_of_mary_in_redemption_1.pdf

Iraeneus, St. "Adversus Haereses," Accessed on 5th Feb 2019. http://www.newadvent.org/fathers/0103322.htm

Jerome, St. "Letter 22 To Eustochium". Accessed 5th Feb 2019. http://www.newadvent.org/fathers/3001022.htm

John Paul II, Pope, St. "Homily at Sanctuary of Our Lady of Guayaquil", Jan 31 1985, *L'Osservatore Romano*, English edition, March 11, 1985.

John Paul II, Pope ."Redemptoris Mater". In *The Encyclicals of John Paul II,* edited by J. Michael Miller, 354-410. Indiana, Our Sunday Visitor Publishing Division, 1996.

Kolbe, St. Maximilian. *Scritti*, Rome, 1997, as quoted in, Miravalle, Dr. Mark. *With Jesus - The story of Mary Co-Redemptrix*. Goleta CA, Queenship Publishing, 2003.

Leo XIII, Pope. "Jucunda Semper", 1894. Accessed 9th April 2019. http://w2.vatican.va/content/leo-xiii/la/encyclicals/documents/hf_l-xiii_enc_08091894_iucunda-semper-expectatione.html

Liguori, St. Alphonsus. *The Glories of Mary*. London, Burns, Oates & Washbourne Ltd, 1868.

L'Osservatore Romano, English edition, as sourced in Miravalle, Dr. Mark. *Mary, Coredemptrix, Mediatrix, Advocate - Theological Foundations. Vol II*. Santa Barbara CA, Queenship Publishing Company, 1996.

L'Osservatore Romano, English edition, as sourced in Miravalle, Dr. Mark. *With Jesus - The story of Mary Co-Redemptrix*. Goleta CA, Queenship Publishing, 2003.

Marie-Dominique Phillippe, Fr. *Mystery of Mary - Mary, Model of the growth of Christian Life.* Houston, Texas, Capital Printing.

Mezard, Rev. *St. Thomas Aquinas Meditations.* Columbus Ohio, College Book Co, 1940.

Miravalle, Dr Mark. *Mary - Coredemptrix, Mediatrix, Advocate - Theological Foundations. Vol I*. Santa Barbara CA, Queenship Publishing Company, 1995.

Miravalle, Dr. Mark. *Mary, Coredemptrix, Mediatrix, Advocate - Theological Foundations. Vol II*. Santa

Barbara CA, Queenship Publishing Company, 1996.

Miravalle, Dr Mark. "Mary in the Early Church." Accessed 5th Feb 2019. http://www.piercedhearts.org/hearts_jesus_mary/heart_mary/mary_early_church_miravalle.htm.

Miravalle, Dr. Mark. *With Jesus - The story of Mary Co-Redemptrix*. Goleta CA, Queenship Publishing, 2003.

Most, Fr William. "Mary's Immaculate Conception", Accessed 13th March 2019. https://www.ewtn.com/faith/teachings/marya2.htm

Neubert, Fr Emil. *Mary in Doctrine*. Milkwaukee, Bruce Publishing Company,1954.

Nyssa, St. Gregory of. *Sermon for the Nativity of Christ*, as sourced in Miravalle, Dr Mark. *Mary - Coredemptrix, Mediatrix, Advocate - Theological Foundations. Vol I*. Santa Barbara CA, Queenship Publishing Company, 1995.

O'Carroll, Rev. Michael. *Mediatress of all Graces*. Maryland, Newman Press, 1958.

Ott, Dr. Ludwig. *Fundamentals of Catholic Dogma*. Charlotte, North Carolina, TAN Books, 1974.

Phillippe, Fr. Marie-Dominique. *Mystery of Mary - Mary, Model of the growth of Christian Life.* Houston, Texas, Capital Printing.

Pius IX, Pope. "Ineffabilis Deus", 1854. Accessed on 25th Feb 2019. http://www.papalencyclicals.net/pius09/p9ineff.htm

Pius X, Pope St. "Ad Diem Illum", 1904, 11-18. In *The Papal Encyclicals 1903-1939.* United States of America, The Pierian Press, 1990.

Pius XI, Pope. "Allocution to Pilgrims from Vicenza, Italy." November 30, 1933, *L'Osservatore Romano*, Dec. 1, 1933.

Pius XII, *Ad Coeli Reginam*. Accessed on 13th June 2019. http://w2.vatican.va/content/pius-xii/en/encyclicals/documents/hf_p-xii_enc_11101954_ad-caeli-reginam.html

Roman Missal, The. New Jersey, Catholic Book Publishing Corp, 2011.

Saunders, Fr. William. "The Feast of Our Lady of Sorrows" Accessed 14th March 2019.

https://www.catholiceducation.org/en/culture/catholic-contributions/the-feast-of-our-lady-of-sorrows.html

Scheeben, Rev. *Mariology Volume One*. St Louis MO, B. Herder Book Co, 1954.

Second Vatican Council, "Dogmatic Constitution on the Church - Lumen Gentium". Accessed 28th Feb 2019. http://www.vatican.va/archive/hist_councils/ii_vatican_council/documents/vat-ii_const_19641121_lumen-gentium_en.html

Sermons of St. Bernard on Advent and Christmas. London, R & T Washbourne, Ltd, 1909.

Smith, William and Theophilus Hall, *Smith's English-Latin Dictionary*. Wauconda, Illinois, Bolchazy-Carducci Publishers Inc, 200.

Tertullian, *De Carne Christi*, as quoted in Dr. Mark Miravalle. *With Jesus - The story of Mary Co-Redemptrix*. Goleta CA, Queenship Publishing, 2003.

Milton Keynes UK
Ingram Content Group UK Ltd.
UKHW011324140324
439518UK00007B/469